THE WEALTH CODE:

Unlocking the Secrets to Billionaire Success

Ricky Dhillon

Get Asia UK

INTRODUCTION

Billionaires - they are the epitome of success and wealth, with fortunes that are beyond most people's wildest dreams. Their success stories inspire awe and admiration, as they demonstrate what is possible when you have a clear vision, the right mindset, and the right strategies.

But what exactly sets billionaires apart from the rest of us? How do they achieve such remarkable success? What secrets do they know that the rest of us don't? These are the questions that this book aims to answer.

"The Wealth Code: Unlocking the Secrets to Billionaire Success" is a comprehensive guide that examines the mindset, strategies, and habits of some of the world's most successful billionaires. Through in-depth analysis and case studies, this book reveals the key factors that have contributed to their success and shows how you can apply these same principles to your own life.

At its core, this book is about unlocking the secrets to success - the principles and strategies that underpin the creation of wealth and the achievement of goals. Whether you're an aspiring entrepreneur, a seasoned business owner, or simply someone looking to improve your financial situation, this book offers practical advice and insights that can help you achieve your goals.

One of the key themes of this book is the mindset of a billionaire. Billionaires think differently from most people, and it is this mindset that has enabled them to achieve such incredible success. This book examines the beliefs, values, and attitudes that billionaires have in common, and shows how you can adopt these same mindsets to achieve your own success.

Another important theme of this book is the importance of networks. Billionaires know that success is not achieved alone - it requires collaboration, partnerships, and a strong network of contacts. This book explores how billionaires build and maintain their networks, and shows how you can do the same.

The book also explores the art of negotiation, a skill that is essential for anyone looking to create wealth. Negotiation is not just about getting the best deal - it's about creating win-win situations that benefit all parties involved. This book examines the negotiation strategies used by billionaires and shows how you can apply them to your own life.

In addition to these themes, the book covers a wide range of topics related to wealth creation, including innovation, risk management, investing, resilience, work-life balance, and giving back to society. Each chapter offers practical advice, real-world examples, and actionable insights that can help you achieve your goals and create the life you desire.

Ultimately, this book is about unlocking the wealth code - the set of principles and strategies that enable billionaires to create massive wealth and achieve incredible success. By studying the strategies of billionaires and applying these same principles to your own life, you too can achieve your goals, build wealth, and create the life you desire.

Whether you're an aspiring entrepreneur, a seasoned business owner, or simply someone looking to improve your financial situation, "The Wealth Code: Unlocking the Secrets to Billionaire Success" offers practical advice and insights that can help you achieve your goals and create the life you desire.

PREFACE

Are you ready to unlock the secrets to billionaire success? Look no further than "The Wealth Code: Unlocking the Secrets to Billionaire Success." This book is a must-read for anyone looking to achieve financial success, and it is jam-packed with practical tips and advice from the world's most successful billionaires.

Discover the mindset of a billionaire and learn how to adopt their thoughts and beliefs to transform your life. Identify your unique value proposition and leverage it to create wealth, and explore the power of networks to build a strong network of contacts and collaborators to create opportunities for wealth creation.

Learn from the best and examine negotiation strategies used by billionaires and how to apply them in your own life. Explore how billionaires come up with new ideas and develop them into successful businesses, and examine how billionaires approach risk management and how to apply their strategies to your own financial decision-making.

Gain insights into the investment strategies of billionaires and learn how to build a strong, diversified investment portfolio. Discover how to build resilience in the face of setbacks and failure, and turn them into opportunities for growth and learning.

Examine how billionaires balance work, family, and personal life to achieve long-term success and fulfillment, and explore how billionaires use their wealth and influence to make a positive impact on society and leave a lasting legacy.

Don't miss out on this incredible opportunity to learn from the best and unlock the secrets to billionaire success. Order your copy of "The Wealth Code" today!

CONTENTS

society and leave a lasting legacy.

CHAPTER 1: THE MINDSET OF A BILLIONAIRE

Examining the thoughts and beliefs that separate billionaires from the rest of us.

Billionaires are a rare breed of individuals who have achieved massive success in their respective fields. They have built empires, created innovative products and services, and changed the world in significant ways. But what sets billionaires apart from the rest of us? Is it their wealth? Their intelligence? Their work ethic?

While these factors undoubtedly play a role in their success, the key differentiator is their mindset. Billionaires think differently from most people, and it is this mindset that has enabled them to achieve such incredible success. In this chapter, we will explore the beliefs, values, and attitudes that billionaires have in common, and show how you can adopt these same mindsets to achieve your own success.

One of the core mindsets of billionaires is a strong sense of purpose. They have a clear vision of what they want to achieve, and they are willing to work tirelessly to make that vision a reality. They are driven by a sense of mission and purpose, and this gives them the energy and motivation they need to overcome any obstacles that come their way.

Billionaires also have an unwavering belief in themselves and their abilities. They know that they have what it takes to achieve their goals, and they are not afraid to take risks and push themselves outside of their comfort zones. This self-belief is essential for success, as it gives them the confidence to pursue their dreams and persevere through challenges.

Another key mindset of billionaires is a focus on opportunity rather than scarcity. While many people see the world as a limited pie, billionaires see a world of limitless possibilities. They are constantly seeking out new opportunities and ways to create value, rather than focusing on what they don't have or what they can't do.

Billionaires also have a growth mindset, which means that they believe that their abilities and intelligence can be developed over time. They view challenges as opportunities for growth and learning, and are not afraid to fail or make mistakes along the way. This mindset allows them to take risks and experiment with new ideas, knowing that they will learn from their experiences and grow as a result.

Finally, billionaires have an abundance mindset when it comes to money. They believe that there is enough wealth to go around, and that their success does not come at the expense of others. They are generous with their wealth and are often philanthropic, using their resources to make a positive impact on the world.

In order to adopt these mindsets, it is important to be intentional about your thinking and to cultivate a growth mindset. This means embracing challenges and setbacks as opportunities for growth, and believing that your abilities and intelligence can be developed over time. It also means focusing on opportunities rather than limitations, and developing a sense of purpose and mission that gives you the energy and motivation you need to pursue your goals.

In conclusion, the mindset of a billionaire is one of the key factors that separates them from the rest of us. They have a clear sense of purpose, unwavering self-belief, a focus on opportunity rather than scarcity, and a growth mindset that allows them to embrace challenges and failures as opportunities for growth. By adopting these same mindsets, you can unlock your full potential and achieve the success you desire.

CHAPTER 2: IDENTIFYING YOUR UNIQUE VALUE PROPOSITION

Determining what sets you apart and how to leverage it to create wealth

In the world of business and entrepreneurship, having a unique value proposition is critical to success. Your value proposition is what sets you apart from your competitors and defines what you offer to your customers or clients. It is what makes you unique, valuable, and desirable. In this chapter, we will explore how to identify your unique value proposition, and how to leverage it to create wealth.

Step 1: Identify Your Strengths

The first step in identifying your unique value proposition is to identify your strengths. What are you good at? What unique skills or talents do you possess? What experiences have you had that have shaped your perspective and approach to the world? Take the time to reflect on your strengths and write them down.

Step 2: Identify Your Target Market

The next step is to identify your target market. Who are you trying to serve? Who is your ideal customer or client? What are their needs, wants, and desires? Understanding your target market is critical to developing a value proposition that resonates with them.

Step 3: Define Your Value Proposition

Now that you understand your strengths and your target market, it's time to define your value proposition. Your value proposition should answer the following questions:

- What unique benefit do you provide to your target market?

- How do you solve their problems or meet their needs?

- What makes you different from your competitors?

Your value proposition should be clear, concise, and focused on the benefits you provide to your target market. It should communicate what sets you apart and why your customers or clients should choose you over your competitors.

Step 4: Test and Refine Your Value Proposition

Once you have developed your value proposition, it's time to test it out. Share it with your target market and gather feedback. Ask them if they understand what you offer and why it's valuable. Ask them if they would choose you over your competitors.

Based on the feedback you receive, refine your value proposition as needed. Make sure it is clear, compelling, and resonates with your target market.

Step 5: Leverage Your Value Proposition to Create Wealth

Once you have developed a clear and compelling value proposition, it's time to leverage it to create wealth. Here are a few ways to do that:

1. Develop a business plan: Use your value proposition to develop a business plan that outlines your strategy for success. Identify your target market, develop a marketing plan, and set goals and milestones for your business.

2. Develop a marketing strategy: Use your value proposition to develop a marketing strategy that communicates your unique benefits to your target market. Use social media, content marketing, and other tactics to reach your audience and build your brand.

3. Build partnerships: Look for opportunities to partner with other businesses or individuals who share your values and can help you reach your target market.

4. Focus on delivering value: Keep your focus on delivering value to your customers or clients. If you consistently provide value, you will build a loyal customer base that will support your business for years to come.

In conclusion, identifying your unique value proposition is critical to success in business and entrepreneurship. By identifying your strengths, understanding your target market, and developing a clear and compelling value proposition, you can differentiate yourself from your competitors and create wealth. Leverage your value proposition to develop a business plan, a marketing strategy, build partnerships, and focus on delivering value to your customers or clients.

CHAPTER 3: THE POWER OF NETWORKS

Exploring how to build a strong network of contacts and collaborators to create opportunities for wealth creation.

In the world of business and entrepreneurship, success is often dependent on who you know. Building a strong network of contacts and collaborators can open doors, create opportunities, and help you achieve your goals. In this chapter, we will explore the power of networks and how to build a strong one to create opportunities for wealth creation.

Step 1: Identify Your Goals

Before you begin building your network, it's important to identify your goals. What are you trying to achieve? Who do you need to know to achieve those goals? Understanding your goals will help you identify the types of people you should be connecting with and the types of opportunities you should be seeking.

Step 2: Attend Networking Events

One of the most effective ways to build your network is to attend networking events. Look for events in your industry or niche and attend them regularly. These events provide an opportunity to meet new people, build relationships, and learn from others.

When attending networking events, be sure to bring plenty of business cards and be prepared to introduce yourself and talk about what you do. Make an effort to listen to others and ask questions. Building relationships is about giving as much as it is about receiving, so look for ways to help others and provide value.

Step 3: Join Professional Organizations

Another way to build your network is to join professional organizations. These organizations provide a forum for like-minded individuals to connect, share ideas, and collaborate. They also often offer educational resources and opportunities for professional development.

When joining a professional organization, look for ways to get involved. Volunteer for committees, attend events, and participate in discussions. By actively participating in the organization, you will build relationships and establish yourself as a thought leader in your industry.

Step 4: Leverage Social Media

Social media is another powerful tool for building your network. Platforms like LinkedIn, Twitter, and Instagram provide an opportunity to connect with others in your industry and share your expertise.

When using social media to build your network, be sure to share valuable content and engage with others. Look for opportunities to connect with influencers in your industry and participate in discussions. Building a strong social media presence can help you establish yourself as a thought leader and attract new opportunities.

Step 5: Build Relationships

Ultimately, building a strong network is about building relationships. Take the time to get to know the people in your network, listen to their needs, and look for ways to provide value. By building strong relationships, you will create a network of contacts and collaborators who can help you achieve your goals and create opportunities for wealth creation.

In conclusion, building a strong network is essential to success in business and entrepreneurship. Attend networking events, join professional organizations, leverage social media, and focus on building relationships. By connecting with like-minded individuals and establishing yourself as a thought leader in your industry, you can create opportunities for wealth creation and achieve your goals.

CHAPTER 4: THE ART OF NEGOTIATION

Examining negotiation strategies used by billionaires and how to apply them in your own life.

Negotiation is a crucial skill in the world of business and entrepreneurship. It is essential for closing deals, building partnerships, and creating opportunities for wealth creation. In this chapter, we will examine the negotiation strategies used by billionaires and explore how you can apply them in your own life.

Step 1: Know What You Want

The first step in any negotiation is to know what you want. This requires a clear understanding of your goals and priorities. Take the time to identify your desired outcomes and what you are willing to compromise on. Knowing what you want will give you confidence and clarity during the negotiation process.

Step 2: Research Your Opponent

Before entering a negotiation, it is important to research your opponent. This will help you understand their priorities, interests, and negotiation style. Look for information about their past negotiations, their reputation, and any relevant industry news. This information can help you anticipate their behavior and plan your negotiation strategy.

Step 3: Build Rapport

Building rapport is an important aspect of any negotiation. Take the time to establish a connection with your opponent by finding common ground, asking questions, and listening actively. Building a rapport can help establish trust and create a more productive negotiation environment.

Step 4: Focus on Value

During a negotiation, it is important to focus on value. This means identifying areas where you and your opponent can create mutual benefit. Look for opportunities to create win-win solutions that satisfy both parties' needs. This approach can help create long-term partnerships and lead to future opportunities for wealth creation.

Step 5: Be Prepared to Walk Away

Sometimes, the best negotiation strategy is to be prepared to walk away. This requires a clear understanding of your priorities and what you are willing to compromise on. If you are not getting what you want from the negotiation, be prepared to walk away and explore other opportunities. This approach can help you maintain your leverage and protect your interests.

Step 6: Follow Up

After a negotiation, it is important to follow up. This means confirming any agreements made during the negotiation and establishing next steps. Following up can help ensure that both parties are on the same page and can help establish a foundation for future negotiations and partnerships.

In conclusion, the art of negotiation is a crucial skill for anyone seeking to create wealth in business and entrepreneurship. By knowing what you want, researching your opponent, building rapport, focusing on value, being prepared to walk away, and following up, you can negotiate effectively and create opportunities for success. By examining the negotiation strategies used by billionaires and applying them in your own life, you can develop the skills and mindset necessary for success in the world of business.

CHAPTER 5: INNOVATING FOR SUCCESS

Exploring how billionaires come up with new ideas and develop them into successful businesses.

Innovation is the lifeblood of successful businesses, and billionaires understand this better than anyone. They are constantly searching for new ideas and ways to improve their businesses, and they have developed strategies for turning those ideas into reality. In this chapter, we will explore how billionaires innovate for success and how you can apply those strategies in your own life.

Step 1: Identify a Problem

The first step in any innovation process is to identify a problem. Billionaires are constantly looking for problems to solve, whether it's a gap in the market or an issue within their own businesses. They understand that solving problems is the key to creating value and generating wealth.

Step 2: Brainstorm Solutions

Once a problem has been identified, the next step is to brainstorm solutions. Billionaires use a variety of techniques to come up with ideas, including brainstorming sessions, focus groups, and customer feedback. They understand that innovation requires creativity and collaboration.

Step 3: Prototype and Test

Once potential solutions have been identified, the next step is to prototype and test them. Billionaires understand that the only way to know if an idea will work is to test it in the real world. They are not afraid to fail and understand that failure is often a necessary step on the path to success.

Step 4: Iterate and Refine

Based on the results of testing, billionaires iterate and refine their ideas. They understand that the first version of a product or service is rarely perfect and that continuous improvement is necessary for success. They gather feedback, make adjustments, and test again.

Step 5: Launch and Scale

Once an idea has been refined and tested, the final step is to launch and scale. Billionaires understand that launching a new product or service requires careful planning and execution. They develop marketing strategies, build partnerships, and scale their businesses to meet demand.

In conclusion, innovating for success is a crucial skill for anyone seeking to create wealth in business and entrepreneurship. By identifying problems, brainstorming solutions, prototyping and testing, iterating and refining, and launching and scaling, you can develop innovative ideas and turn them into successful businesses. By examining the strategies used by billionaires and applying them in your own life, you can develop the skills and mindset necessary for success in the world of business.

CHAPTER 6:
MANAGING RISK

Examining how billionaires approach risk management and how to apply their strategies to your own financial decision-making.

Billionaires are often seen as risk-takers, but the truth is that they are also experts at managing risk. They understand that taking calculated risks is necessary for creating wealth, but they also know that managing those risks is essential for avoiding catastrophic losses. In this chapter, we will examine how billionaires approach risk management and how you can apply their strategies to your own financial decision-making.

Step 1: Identify and Assess Risk

The first step in risk management is to identify and assess the risks involved in a particular investment or business venture. Billionaires use a variety of tools and techniques to assess risk, including financial analysis, market research, and expert opinions. They understand that a thorough understanding of the risks involved is essential for making informed decisions.

Step 2: Develop a Risk Management Plan

Once the risks have been identified and assessed, the next step is to develop a risk management plan. This plan should outline the steps that will be taken to mitigate the risks involved in the investment or business venture. Billionaires use a variety of risk management strategies, including diversification, hedging, and insurance. They understand that a comprehensive risk management plan can help to minimize losses and protect their wealth.

Step 3: Monitor and Adjust

Risk management is not a one-time event; it is an ongoing process. Billionaires understand that the risks involved in an investment or business venture can change over time, and that it is essential to monitor and adjust the risk management plan accordingly. They use a variety of tools and techniques to monitor risk, including financial reports, market analysis, and expert opinions.

Step 4: Be Prepared for the Unexpected

Despite the best risk management plans, unexpected events can still occur. Billionaires understand that being prepared for the unexpected is essential for managing risk. They maintain a cash reserve, build strong relationships with lenders and investors, and develop contingency plans to mitigate the impact of unexpected events.

Step 5: Embrace Risk

Finally, billionaires understand that taking calculated risks is necessary for creating wealth. They do not shy away from risk, but rather embrace it and use it to their advantage. They understand that by taking calculated risks, they can achieve greater returns and create opportunities for growth and innovation.

In conclusion, managing risk is a crucial skill for anyone seeking to create wealth in business and entrepreneurship. By identifying and assessing risks, developing a risk management plan, monitoring and adjusting, being prepared for the unexpected, and embracing risk, you can develop a comprehensive risk management strategy that can help to protect your wealth and create opportunities for growth and innovation. By examining the strategies used by billionaires and applying them in your own financial decision-making, you can develop the skills and mindset necessary for success in the world of business.

CHAPTER 7:
INVESTING FOR
THE LONG-TERM

Discussing the investment strategies of billionaires and how to build a strong, diversified investment portfolio.

Billionaires have accumulated their wealth through a variety of means, including entrepreneurship, innovation, and investment. Investing is an essential component of wealth creation, and billionaires have developed a range of investment strategies that have helped them to achieve long-term financial success. In this chapter, we will discuss the investment strategies of billionaires and explore how you can build a strong, diversified investment portfolio.

Diversification is Key

One of the most important investment strategies employed by billionaires is diversification. Diversification means spreading your investments across multiple asset classes, sectors, and geographies to reduce risk and increase potential returns. Billionaires understand that diversification is key to building a strong, resilient investment portfolio.

Investing in Equities

Billionaires often invest heavily in equities, or stocks. Stocks represent ownership in a company and offer the potential for long-term capital appreciation. Billionaires typically invest in a mix of blue-chip, growth, and value stocks to achieve a balance of stability and growth. They also invest in international stocks to diversify their portfolios across different geographies.

Investing in Bonds

Bonds are debt securities that offer a fixed income over a specified period. Billionaires often invest in high-quality corporate and government bonds as a means of diversifying their portfolios and generating regular income. They also use bonds as a hedge against stock market volatility.

Real Estate Investing

Billionaires have long understood the value of real estate investing. Real estate offers the potential for capital appreciation and regular income from rent. Billionaires often invest in a mix of residential and commercial real estate to diversify their portfolios. They also look for opportunities to add value to their properties through renovations and development.

Alternative Investments

Billionaires often invest in alternative assets such as private equity, hedge funds, and venture capital. These investments offer the potential for high returns but also come with higher risk. Billionaires typically allocate a portion of their portfolios to alternative investments to achieve a balance of risk and return.

Investing for the Long-Term

Billionaires understand that investing for the long-term is essential for building wealth. They take a disciplined approach to investing, focusing on the fundamentals of the companies they invest in and avoiding short-term market fluctuations. They also prioritize saving and investing early in their careers to take advantage of the power of compounding over time.

In conclusion, building a strong, diversified investment portfolio is essential for long-term financial success. Billionaires have developed a range of investment strategies that have helped them to achieve wealth over time. Diversification, investing in equities and bonds, real estate investing, and alternative investments are all key components of a strong investment portfolio. By following the investment strategies of billionaires and taking a disciplined approach to investing, you can build wealth over time and achieve financial independence.

CHAPTER 8:
DEVELOPING
RESILIENCE

Exploring how to build resilience in the face of setbacks and failure, and turn them into opportunities for growth and learning.

Billionaires face setbacks and failures just like anyone else. However, what sets them apart is their ability to bounce back from these setbacks and turn them into opportunities for growth and learning. Resilience is a key trait that is essential for success in any field. In this chapter, we will explore how to build resilience and develop the mental toughness necessary to overcome adversity and achieve success.

The Importance of Resilience

Resilience is the ability to bounce back from setbacks and continue moving forward. It is an essential trait for success in any field, as setbacks and failures are inevitable. Billionaires understand the importance of resilience and have developed the mental toughness necessary to overcome adversity and achieve success.

Cultivating a Growth Mindset

One of the key ways to build resilience is to cultivate a growth mindset. A growth mindset is the belief that one's abilities and intelligence can be developed through hard work and dedication. Billionaires understand that setbacks and failures are opportunities for growth and learning. They view challenges as a chance to improve themselves and their businesses.

Learning from Setbacks and Failure

Billionaires also understand the importance of learning from setbacks and failure. They do not see failures as a reflection of their worth or ability. Instead, they view them as an opportunity to learn from their mistakes and make improvements. They take a systematic approach to analyzing their failures, looking for ways to improve their processes and strategies.

Maintaining a Positive Attitude

Maintaining a positive attitude is another key component of resilience. Billionaires understand that maintaining a positive attitude, even in the face of setbacks and failure, can help them to stay motivated and focused on their goals. They surround themselves with positive people who support their vision and believe in their ability to succeed.

Developing a Support Network

Having a strong support network is also essential for building resilience. Billionaires understand that they cannot achieve success alone. They surround themselves with people who support their vision and provide them with guidance and feedback. They also seek out mentors who can offer them advice and help them to navigate the challenges of entrepreneurship.

In conclusion, building resilience is essential for success in any field, including entrepreneurship. Billionaires understand the importance of resilience and have developed the mental toughness necessary to overcome setbacks and failures. Cultivating a growth mindset, learning from setbacks and failure, maintaining a positive attitude, and developing a support network are all key components of resilience. By developing these traits and strategies, you can build the mental toughness necessary to overcome adversity and achieve success.

CHAPTER 9: LIVING A BALANCED LIFE

Examining how billionaires balance work, family, and personal life to achieve long-term success and fulfillment.

Billionaires are known for their intense work ethic and dedication to their businesses. However, they also understand the importance of maintaining a balanced life. In this chapter, we will examine how billionaires balance work, family, and personal life to achieve long-term success and fulfillment.

The Importance of Work-Life Balance

Work-life balance is essential for long-term success and fulfillment. It allows individuals to maintain their physical and mental health, build strong relationships with family and friends, and pursue personal interests and hobbies. Billionaires understand the importance of work-life balance and strive to maintain a healthy balance between their work and personal lives.

Prioritizing Family and Relationships

Billionaires understand the importance of strong relationships and prioritize their family and personal relationships. They make time for their spouses, children, and close friends, and they understand the importance of maintaining these relationships over the long-term. They also recognize the value of having a strong support network and building relationships with mentors and other successful entrepreneurs.

Delegating Responsibility

Billionaires also understand the importance of delegating responsibility. They recognize that they cannot do everything themselves and that they need to trust others to handle certain tasks and responsibilities. By delegating responsibility, billionaires are able to focus on the tasks that are most important to the success of their businesses and their personal lives.

Pursuing Personal Interests and Hobbies

Billionaires also recognize the importance of pursuing personal interests and hobbies. They understand that taking time for themselves can help them to recharge their batteries and maintain their mental and physical health. They pursue activities that they enjoy, whether it's playing a sport, traveling, or pursuing a creative hobby.

Managing Stress and Burnout

Finally, billionaires understand the importance of managing stress and burnout. They recognize that they are only human and that they need to take care of themselves in order to maintain their productivity and creativity. They take breaks when they need them, whether it's taking a vacation or simply taking a few hours to relax and recharge.

In conclusion, maintaining a balanced life is essential for long-term success and fulfillment. Billionaires understand the importance of work-life balance and strive to maintain a healthy balance between their work and personal lives. They prioritize their family and personal relationships, delegate responsibility, pursue personal interests and hobbies, and manage stress and burnout. By following these strategies, you can achieve long-term success and fulfillment in both your personal and professional life.

CHAPTER 10: GIVING BACK TO SOCIETY –

Exploring how billionaires use their wealth and influence to make a positive impact on society and leave a lasting legacy.

Billionaires not only amass great wealth and success, but they also have a responsibility to use their influence to create a positive impact on society. In this chapter, we will explore how billionaires give back to society and use their wealth and influence to make a difference in the world.

Philanthropy

One of the most common ways billionaires give back to society is through philanthropy. Billionaires donate millions and sometimes billions of dollars to charitable causes, foundations, and organizations. Philanthropy allows billionaires to create a lasting impact on society and address important issues such as poverty, education, and healthcare.

Many billionaires also create their own foundations to support causes that are important to them. These foundations fund research, education, and community programs, and they can make a significant impact on the world.

Social Entrepreneurship

Another way billionaires give back to society is through social entrepreneurship. Social entrepreneurs use business strategies to address social and environmental issues. They create businesses that have a social or environmental mission, and they use their profits to reinvest in their communities.

Social entrepreneurship can create jobs, improve access to education and healthcare, and address issues such as climate change and inequality. Billionaire social entrepreneurs such as Elon Musk, Richard Branson, and Bill Gates have created businesses that have a significant positive impact on society.

Political Activism

Billionaires also use their wealth and influence to create change through political activism. They fund political campaigns and support candidates who share their values and beliefs. They also use their influence to push for policy changes that align with their goals.

Political activism can be controversial, and billionaires who engage in political activism often face criticism. However, they believe that they have a responsibility to use their wealth and influence to create positive change in society.

Corporate Social Responsibility

Finally, billionaires can also give back to society through corporate social responsibility. Corporate social responsibility refers to the responsibility of businesses to make a positive impact on society and the environment. Many billionaires run large businesses, and they have the ability to make a significant impact through corporate social responsibility initiatives.

Corporate social responsibility can take many forms, such as reducing carbon emissions, creating fair labor practices, and supporting community programs. Billionaire entrepreneurs such as Jeff Bezos and Mark Zuckerberg have created large-scale corporate social responsibility programs that make a significant positive impact on society.

In conclusion, billionaires have a responsibility to use their wealth and influence to create a positive impact on society. They can give back through philanthropy, social entrepreneurship, political activism, and corporate social responsibility. By giving back, billionaires can create a lasting legacy and make a significant impact on the world.

CONCLUSION

In this book, we have explored the strategies and mindsets that have helped billionaires achieve extraordinary success. From identifying your unique value proposition to investing for the long-term, each chapter has provided valuable insights and actionable tips for building wealth and creating a fulfilling life.

One recurring theme throughout the book is the mindset of a billionaire. We have seen how billionaires think differently from most people, focusing on opportunities rather than obstacles and taking calculated risks to achieve their goals. By adopting this mindset, we too can unlock our full potential and create the life we desire.

Another key takeaway is the power of networks. Building strong relationships and collaborating with others can open doors and create opportunities that we may not have otherwise. By following the tips and strategies outlined in this book, we can cultivate a valuable network of contacts and collaborators to create wealth and achieve our goals.

Negotiation is another critical skill that separates billionaires from the rest of us. By understanding the negotiation strategies used by billionaires, we can apply them in our own lives to get what we want and create win-win situations for ourselves and others.

We have also explored the importance of innovation in

creating successful businesses. By coming up with new ideas and developing them into marketable products or services, billionaires have been able to build empires and change the world. By fostering our own creativity and innovation, we too can find success and make a lasting impact.

Managing risk is another crucial aspect of wealth creation that we have covered in this book. Billionaires take calculated risks and manage them carefully, minimizing their downside while maximizing their potential gains. By applying their strategies to our own financial decision-making, we can protect ourselves from unnecessary risks and increase our chances of success.

Investing for the long-term is another skill that billionaires have mastered. By diversifying their portfolios and focusing on long-term growth, they have been able to build substantial wealth over time. By following their investment strategies, we too can build a strong financial foundation for ourselves and our families.

Building resilience is another important trait that billionaires possess. By embracing failure and turning setbacks into opportunities for growth and learning, they have been able to overcome obstacles and achieve success. By developing our own resilience, we can learn to bounce back from adversity and emerge stronger than before.

Achieving a balanced life is another critical aspect of billionaire success. By balancing work, family, and personal life, billionaires have been able to achieve long-term success and fulfillment. By following their example, we too can create a life that is fulfilling and meaningful.

Finally, we have explored how billionaires use their wealth and influence to make a positive impact on society and leave a lasting legacy. By giving back to society, they have been able to make a difference in the world and leave a positive mark on history. By finding our own ways to give back, we too can make a difference and leave a lasting legacy.

In conclusion, the strategies and mindsets outlined in this book can help anyone achieve extraordinary success and create a fulfilling life. By adopting the mindset of a billionaire, building strong networks, negotiating effectively, innovating for success, managing risk, investing for the long-term, building resilience, achieving balance, and giving back, we can unlock our full potential and create a life that is both rich in wealth and in meaning.

EPILOGUE

As we conclude this journey through the secrets to billionaire success, it is important to reflect on the key takeaways and insights gained from examining the various topics covered in this book.

The mindset of a billionaire is one that is focused on abundance, growth, and possibility. By cultivating a positive and proactive mindset, you too can unlock your full potential and achieve extraordinary success.

Identifying your unique value proposition is essential to creating wealth. By understanding what sets you apart and leveraging it to your advantage, you can build a strong foundation for success.

The power of networks cannot be overstated. Building a strong network of contacts and collaborators can create opportunities for wealth creation and help you achieve your goals faster.

Negotiation is a skill that can be learned and mastered. By examining the strategies used by billionaires and applying them in your own life, you can become a more effective negotiator and achieve better outcomes in your financial decisions.

Innovation is the lifeblood of successful businesses. By coming up with new ideas and developing them into viable ventures, you can create a lasting impact and achieve great success.

Risk management is a critical aspect of wealth creation. By examining how billionaires approach risk and applying their strategies to your own financial decision-making, you can mitigate risk and increase your chances of success.

Investing for the long-term is essential to building a strong, diversified investment portfolio. By adopting the investment strategies of billionaires, you can achieve long-term growth and financial security.

Developing resilience is key to bouncing back from setbacks and failures. By embracing a growth mindset and turning setbacks into opportunities for growth and learning, you can achieve greater success and fulfillment.

Balancing work, family, and personal life is essential to achieving long-term success and fulfillment. By examining how billionaires achieve balance and applying their strategies in your own life, you can achieve greater happiness and well-being.

Finally, giving back to society is a hallmark of billionaire success. By using your wealth and influence to make a positive impact on society, you can leave a lasting legacy and achieve a sense of purpose and fulfillment.

In conclusion, by mastering the secrets to billionaire success outlined in this book, you can unlock your full potential, achieve extraordinary success, and make a positive impact on the world around you.

AFTERWORD

Congratulations, you've made it to the end of The Wealth Code: Unlocking the Secrets to Billionaire Success. I hope that this book has provided you with valuable insights and practical strategies for achieving success and wealth in your own life.

Throughout this book, we have examined the key principles and practices that billionaires use to create and sustain their wealth. We've explored topics such as mindset, identifying your unique value proposition, the power of networks, negotiation, innovation, risk management, investing, resilience, balancing work and life, and giving back to society.

But remember, success and wealth are not just about accumulating material possessions or financial assets. It's also about making a positive impact on the world around us and leaving a lasting legacy.

So, as you continue on your journey to success and wealth, keep in mind that it's not just about what you can gain, but also what you can give back. Use your wealth and influence to make a positive impact on society and leave a lasting legacy that you can be proud of.

I encourage you to continue learning, growing, and applying the principles and practices outlined in this book. And always remember, success and wealth are within your reach if you have the right mindset and take consistent action towards your goals.

Thank you for taking the time to read The Wealth Code. I wish you all the best on your journey to success and wealth.